Canadian Intellectual Property Office
Registration Number: 1214408, Registered on 22 JUN 2024
ISBN: 979-8-89496-263-4
Written by: Edward Shammas
Linktree: https://linktr.ee/eabsh
Email: eabshammas@gmail.com
Illustrations/Book layout : Mayssa Kennouche
Website: https://mayssakennouche.com/
For permissions, contact:
Edward Shammas

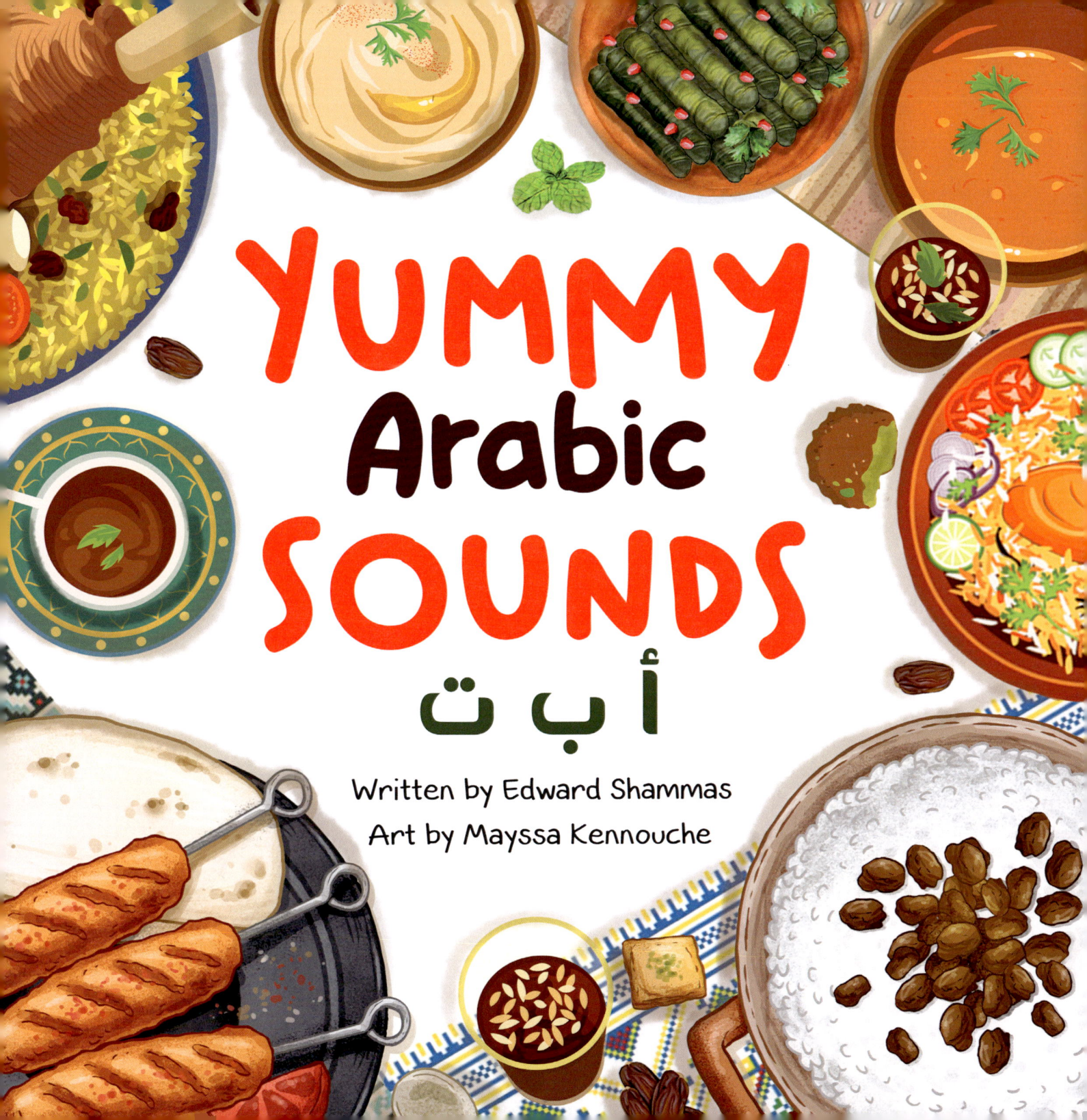

YUMMY Arabic SOUNDS

أ ب ت

Written by Edward Shammas

Art by Mayssa Kennouche

ALiF

س	ا	ن	ا	ن	أ

A-NA-NAS

BAA

ب

ب	ق	ل	ا	و	ة

BAQ-LA-WA

TAA

ت م ر

TA-MR

THAA

ث م ا ر

ا ل ب ح ر

THI-MAR AL-BAHR

JEEM

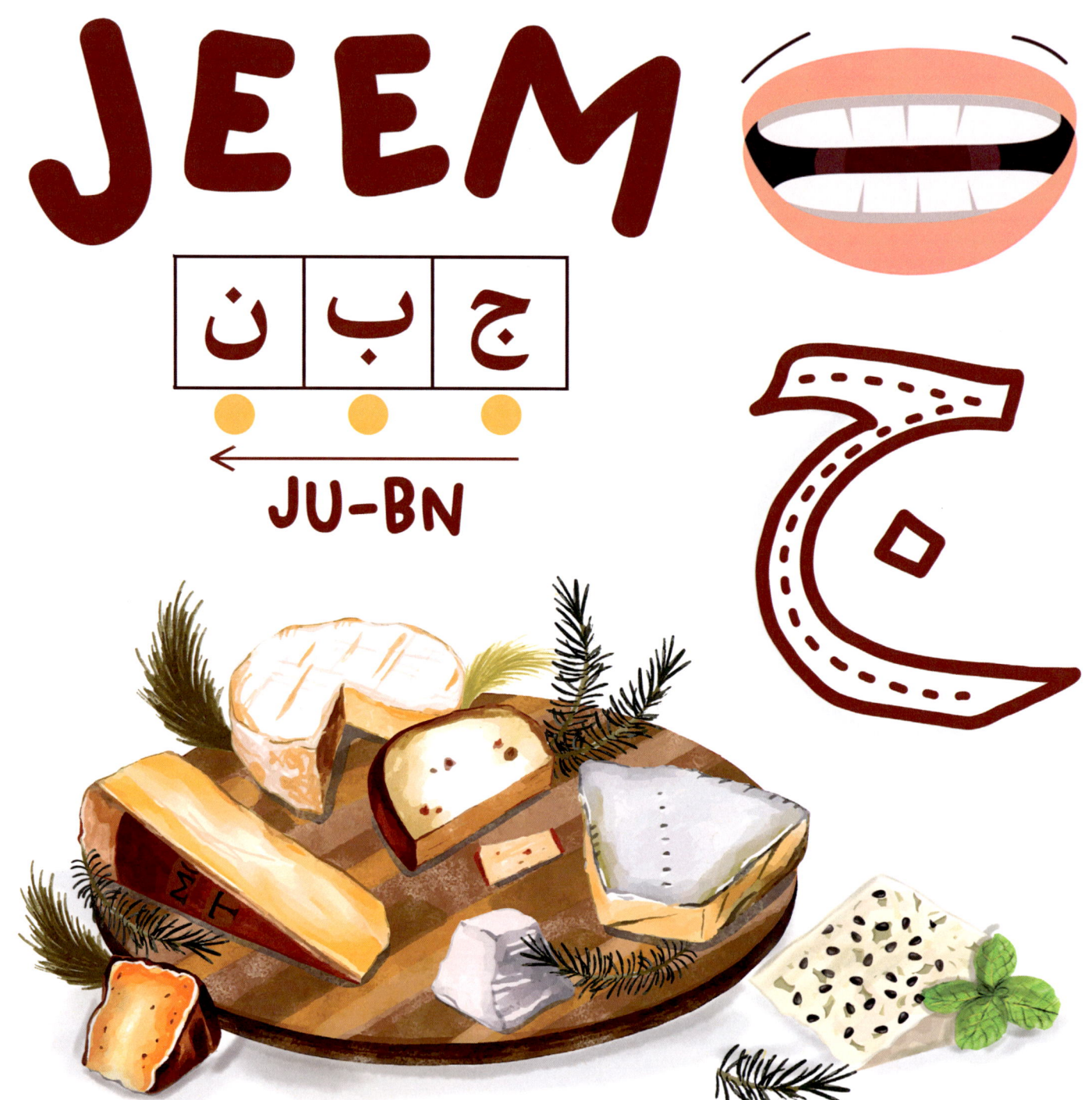

ن	ب	ج

← JU-BN

HAA

حــ صم ح

HUM-MUS

KHAA

خ ب ز

KHO-BZ

DAAL

ج | ا | ج | د

DA-JA-J

DHAAL

ذ ر	ر	ة

DHU-RA

ذ

RAA

Rice

ر ز ر

RU-Z

SEEN

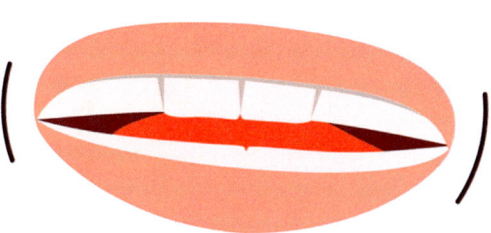

ك	م	س

SA-MAK

SHEEN

ش

ة	ب	ر	و	ش

SH-OR-BA

SAAD

ص

ر	ب	و	ن	ص

SA-NAW-BAR

DHAAD

ة	ف	ا	ي	ض

د	ي	ع	ل	ا

ض

DI-YAA-FAT AL-EED

TAA

ي	ش	ر	ط

TUR-SHEE

ط

DHAA

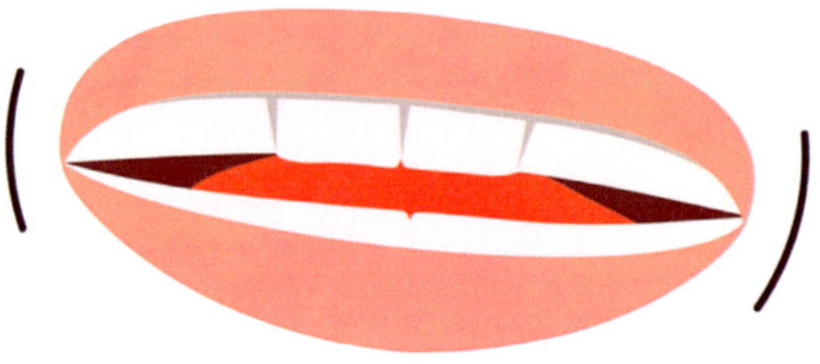

ة	ر	ف	ظ

THF-RA

AYN

ع

عصير

A-SEER

GHAYN

غ

ل	ز	غ

ت	ا	ن	ب	ل	ا

GHA-ZL AL-BA-NAT

FAA

ا	ي	ل	و	ص	ا	ف

FA-SOO-LYA

QAAF

ق

ق	ط	ا	ي	ف

QA-TA-YEF

KAAF

ك ب ة

← KIB-BEH

لك

LAAM

ل

م	ح	ل

ن	ي	ج	ع	ب

LA-HM B-AJEEN

MEEM

م	ش	ا	و	ي

MA-SHA-WEE

NOON

ن

عَ	ا	نَ	عَ	نَ

← NAA-NAA

HAA

ل	ي	ه

HAY-L

WAAW

ق	ر	و
🔴	🔴	🔴

←

ب	ن	ع
🔴	🔴	🔴

←

WA-RAQ E-NAB

YAA

ي

ن ي ط ق ي

YA-Q-TEEN

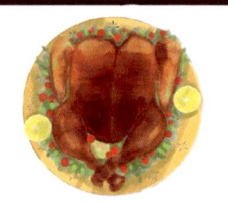

دجاج
DAJAJ

خبز
KHOBZ

حمص
HUMMUS

جبن
JUBN

طرشي
TURSHEE

ضيافة العيد
DIYAAFAT AL EED

صنوبر
SANAWBAR

شوربة
SHORBA

مشاوي
MASHAWEE

لحم بعجين
LAHM BAJEEN

كبة
KIBBEH

قطايف
QATAYEF

يقطين
YAQTEEN

ورق عنب
WARAQ ENAB

ثمار البحر
THIMAR AL BAHR

تمر
TAMR

بقلاوة
BAQLAWA

أناناس
ANANAS

سمك
SAMAK

زعتر
ZAATAR

رز
RUZ

ذرة
DHURA

فاصوليا
FASOOLYA

غزل البنات
GHAZL AL BANAT

عصير
ASEER

ظفرة
THFRA

هيل
HAYL

نعناع
NAANAA

www.ingramcontent.com/pod-product-compliance
Lightning Source LLC
Chambersburg PA
CBRC090830120626
46547CB00008B/642